THE BOOK OF THE LAW

THE BOOK OF THE LAW

[technically called

LIBER
AL vel
LEGIS

SUB FIGURA

CCXX

AS DELIVERED BY

XCIII = 418

TO

DCLXVI]

An Ixii Sol in Aries March 21, 1938 e.v.

Privately issued by the O.T.O.
BCM/ANKH
188, High Holborn, London, W.C.1.

WEISER BOOKS
Boston, MA/York Beach, ME

This edition of *The Book of the Law*
Fisrt published in 1976 by
Red Wheel/Weiser, LLC
York Beach, ME
With offices at:
368 Congress Street
Boston, MA 02210
www.redwheelweiser.com

07 06 05 04
22 21 20 19

The introduction and text have been photo-offset from the 1938 London edition
published by the O.T.O., with corrections.

For doubtful spellings and styles consult the facimile MSS reproduced at the end
of this volume.

Copyright © 1938 Ordo Templi Orientis
O. T. O. International Headquarters
Postfach 332012, D-1418
Berlin, Germany

ISBN 0-87728-334-6
TCP

Printed in Canada

INTRODUCTION.

I.

THE BOOK.

1. This book was dictated in Cairo between noon and 1 p.m. on three successive days, April 8th, 9th and 10th in the year 1904.

The Author called himself Aiwass, and claimed to be " the minister of Hoor-paar-kraat " ; that is, a messenger from the forces ruling this earth at present, as will be explained later on.

How could he prove that he was in fact a being of a kind superior to any of the human race, and so entitled to speak with authority? Evidently he must show KNOWLEDGE and POWER such as no man has ever been known to possess.

2. He showed his KNOWLEDGE chiefly by the use of cipher or cryptogram in certain passages to set forth recondite facts, including some events which had yet to take place, such that no human being could possibly be aware of them ; thus, the proof of his claim exists in the manuscript itself. It is independent of any human witness.

The study of these passages necessarily demands supreme human scholarship to interpret— it needs years of intense application. A great deal has still to be worked out. But enough has been discovered to justify his claim ; the most sceptical intelligence is compelled to admit its truth.

This matter is best studied under the Master Therion, whose years of arduous research have led him to enlightenment.

On the other hand, the language of most of the Book is admirably simple, clear and vigorous. No one can read it without being stricken in the very core of his being.

3. The more than human POWER of Aiwass is shewn by the influence of his Master, and of the Book, upon actual events : and history fully supports the claim made by him. These facts are appreciable by every one ; but are better understood with the help of the Master Therion.

4. The full detailed account of the events leading up to the dictation of this Book, with facsimile reproduction of the Manuscript and an essay by the Master Therion, is published in *The Equinox of the Gods*.

II.

THE UNIVERSE.

This Book explains the Universe.

The elements are Nuit—Space—that is, the total of possibilities of every kind—and Hadit, any point which has experience of these possibilities. (This idea is for literary convenience symbolized by the Egyptian Goddess Nuit, a woman bending over like the Arch of the Night Sky. Hadit is symbolized as a Winged Globe at the heart of Nuit.)

Every event is a uniting of some one monad with one of the experiences possible to it.

"Every man and every woman is a star," that is, an aggregate of such experiences, constantly changing with each fresh event, which affects him or her either consciously or subconsciously.

Each one of us has thus an universe of his own, but it is the same universe for each one as soon as it includes all possible experience. This implies the extension of consciousness to include all other consciousness.

In our present stage, the object that you see is

never the same as the one that I see ; we infer that it is the same because your experience tallies with mine on so many points that the actual differences of our observation are negligible. For instance, if a friend is walking between us, you see only his left side, I his right ; but we agree that it is the same man, although we may differ not only as to what we may see of his body but as to what we know of his qualities. This conviction of identity grows stronger as we see him more often and get to know him better. Yet all the time neither of us can know anything of him at all beyond the total impression made on our respective minds.

The above is an extremely crude attempt to explain a system which reconciles all existing schools of philosophy.

III.

THE LAW OF THELEMA.*

This Book lays down a simple Code of Conduct.
" Do what thou wilt shall be the whole of the
Law."

" Love is the law, love under will."

" There is no law beyond Do what thou wilt."

This means that each of us stars is to move on
our true orbit, as marked out by the nature of our
position, the law of our growth, the impulse of our
past experiences. All events are equally lawful—
and every one necessary, in the long run—for all
of us, in theory ; but in practice, only one act is
lawful for each one of us at any given moment.
Therefore Duty consists in determining to
experience the right event from one moment of
consciousness to another.

Each action or motion is an act of love, the
uniting with one or another part of " Nuit " ;
each such act must be ' under will,' chosen so as to

* Thelema is the Greek for Will, and has the same numerical value
as Agape, the Greek for Love.

9

fulfil and not to thwart the true nature of the being concerned.

The technical methods of achieving this are to be studied in ' Magick,' or acquired by personal instruction from the Master Therion and his appointed assistants.

IV.

THE NEW AEON.

The third chapter of the Book is difficult to understand, and may be very repugnant to many people born before the date of the book (April, 1904).

It tells us the characteristics of the Period on which we are now entered. Superficially, they appear appalling. We see some of them already with terrifying clarity. But fear not !

It explains that certain vast 'stars' (or aggregates of experience) may be described as Gods. One of these is in charge of the destinies of this planet for periods of 2,000 years.* In the history of the world, as far as we know accurately, are three such Gods : Isis, the mother, when the Universe was conceived as simple nourishment drawn directly from her ; this period is marked by matriarchal government.

Next, beginning 500 B.C., Osiris, the father,

---

* The moment of change from one period to another is technically called The Equinox of the Gods.

when the Universe was imagined as catastrophic, love, death, resurrection, as the method by which experience was built up; this corresponds to patriarchal systems.

Now, Horus, the child, in which we come to perceive events as a continual growth partaking in its elements of both these methods, and not to be overcome by circumstance. This present period involves the recognition of the individual as the unit of society.

We realize ourselves as explained in the first paragraphs of this essay. Every event, including death, is only one more accretion to our experience, freely willed by ourselves from the beginning and therefore also predestined.

This " God," Horus, has a technical title : Heru-Ra-Ha, a combination of twin gods, Ra-Hoor-Khuit and Hoor-Paar-Kraat. The meaning of this doctrine must be studied in ' Magick.' (He is symbolized as a Hawk-Headed God enthroned.)

He rules the present period of 2,000 years, beginning in 1904. Everywhere his government is taking root. Observe for yourselves the decay of the sense of sin, the growth of innocence and irresponsibility, the strange modifications of the reproductive instinct with a tendency to become bi-sexual or epicene, the childlike confidence in progress combined with nightmare fear of catastrophe, against which we are yet half unwilling to take precautions.

Consider the outcrop of dictatorships, only possible when moral growth is in its earliest stages, and the prevalence of infantile cults like Communism, Fascism, Pacifism, Health Crazes, Occultism in nearly all its forms, religions sentimentalised to the point of practical extinction.

Consider the popularity of the cinema, the wireless, the football pools and guessing competitions, all devices for soothing fractious infants, no seed of purpose in them.

Consider sport, the babyish enthusiasms and rages which it excites, whole nations disturbed by disputes between boys.

Consider war, the atrocities which occur daily and leave us unmoved and hardly worried.

We are children.

How this new Aeon of Horus will develop, how the Child will grow up, these are for us to determine, growing up ourselves in the way of the Law of Thelema under the enlightened guidance of the Master Therion.

V.

THE NEXT STEP.

Democracy dodders.

Ferocious Fascism, cackling Communism, equally frauds, cavort crazily all over the globe.

They are hemming us in.

They are abortive births of the Child, the New Aeon of Horus.

Liberty stirs once more in the womb of Time.

Evolution makes its changes by anti-Socialistic ways. The 'abnormal' man who foresees the trend of the times and adapts circumstance intelligently, is laughed at, persecuted, often destroyed by the herd; but he and his heirs, when the crisis comes, are survivors.

Above us to-day hangs a danger never yet paralleled in history. We suppress the individual in more and more ways. We think in terms of the herd. War no longer kills soldiers; it kills all indiscriminately. Every new measure of the most democratic and autocratic governments is Communistic in essence. It is always restriction. We are all treated as imbecile children. Dora, the

14

Shops Act, the Motoring Laws, Sunday suffocation, the Censorship—they won't trust us to cross the roads at will.

Fascism is like Communism, and dishonest into the bargain. The dictators suppress all art, literature, theatre, music, news, that does not meet their requirements; yet the world only moves by the light of genius. The herd will be destroyed in mass.

The establishment of the Law of Thelema is the only way to preserve individual liberty and to assure the future of the race.

In the words of the famous paradox of the Comte de Fénix—The absolute rule of the state shall be a function of the absolute liberty of each individual will.

All men and women are invited to co-operate with the Master Therion in this, the Great Work.

O. M.

A∴ A∴ PUBLICATION IN CLASS A.

THE BOOK OF THE LAW

1. Had ! The manifestation of Nuit.

2. The unveiling of the company of heaven.

3. Every man and every woman is a star.

4. Every number is infinite; there is no difference.

5. Help me, o warrior lord of Thebes, in my unveiling before the Children of men !

6. Be thou Hadit, my secret centre, my heart & my tongue !

7. Behold ! it is revealed by Aiwass the minister of Hoor-paar-kraat.

8. The Khabs is in the Khu, not the Khu in the Khabs.

9. Worship then the Khabs, and behold my light shed over you !

10. Let my servants be few & secret : they shall rule the many & the known.

11. These are fools that men adore; both their Gods & their men are fools.

12. Come forth, o children, under the stars, & take your fill of love !

13. I am above you and in you. My ecstasy is in yours. My joy is to see your joy.

14. Above, the gemmèd azure is
    The naked splendour of Nuit ;

> She bends in ecstasy to kiss
>> The secret ardours of Hadit.
> The wingèd globe, the starry blue,
> Are mine, O Ankh-af-na-khonsu !

15. Now ye shall know that the chosen priest & apostle of infinite space is the prince-priest the Beast ; and in his woman called the Scarlet Woman is all power given. They shall gather my children into their fold : they shall bring the glory of the stars into the hearts of men.

16. For he is ever a sun, and she a moon. But to him is the winged secret flame, and to her the stooping starlight.

17. But ye are not so chosen.

18. Burn upon their brows, o splendrous serpent !

19. O azure-lidded woman, bend upon them !

20. The key of the rituals is in the secret word which I have given unto him.

21. With the God & the Adorer I am nothing : they do not see me. They are as upon the earth ; I am Heaven, and there is no other God than me, and my lord Hadit.

22. Now, therefore, I am known to ye by my name Nuit, and to him by a secret name which I will give him when at last he knoweth me. Since

I am Infinite Space, and the Infinite Stars thereof, do ye also thus. Bind nothing! Let there be no difference made among you between any one thing & any other thing; for thereby there cometh hurt.

23. But whoso availeth in this, let him be the chief of all!

24. I am Nuit, and my word is six and fifty.

25. Divide, add, multiply, and understand.

26. Then saith the prophet and slave of the beauteous one : Who am I, and what shall be the sign ? So she answered him, bending down, a lambent flame of blue, all-touching, all penetrant, her lovely hands upon the black earth, & her lithe body arched for love, and her soft feet not hurting the little flowers : Thou knowest ! And the sign shall be my ecstasy, the consciousness of the continuity of existence, the omnipresence of my body.

27. Then the priest answered & said unto the Queen of Space, kissing her lovely brows, and the dew of her light bathing his whole body in a sweet-smelling perfume of sweat : O Nuit, continuous one of Heaven, let it be ever thus ; that men speak not of Thee as One but as None ; and let them speak not of thee at all, since thou art continuous !

28.   None, breathed the light, faint & faery, of the stars, and two.

29.   For I am divided for love's sake, for the chance of union.

30.   This is the creation of the world, that the pain of division is as nothing, and the joy of dissolution all.

31.   For these fools of men and their woes care not thou at all ! They feel little ; what is, is balanced by weak joys ; but ye are my chosen ones.

32.   Obey my prophet ! follow out the ordeals of my knowledge ! seek me only ! Then the joys of my love will redeem ye from all pain. This is so : I swear it by the vault of my body ; by my sacred heart and tongue ; by all I can give, by all I desire of ye all.

33.   Then the priest fell into a deep trance or swoon, & said unto the Queen of Heaven ; Write unto us the ordeals; write unto us the rituals ; write unto us the law !

34.   But she said : the ordeals I write not : the rituals shall be half known and half concealed : the Law is for all.

35.   This that thou writest is the threefold book of Law.

36. My scribe Ankh-af-na-khonsu, the priest of the princes, shall not in one letter change this book ; but lest there be folly, he shall comment thereupon by the wisdom of Ra-Hoor-Khu-it.

37. Also the mantras and spells ; the obeah and the wanga ; the work of the wand and the work of the sword ; these he shall learn and teach.

38. He must teach ; but he may make severe the ordeals.

39. The word of the Law is $\theta\epsilon\lambda\eta\mu\alpha$.

40. Who calls us Thelemites will do no wrong, if he look but close into the word. For there are therein Three Grades, the Hermit, and the Lover, and the man of Earth. Do what thou wilt shall be the whole of the Law.

41. The word of Sin is Restriction. O man ! refuse not thy wife, if she will ! O lover, if thou wilt, depart ! There is no bond that can unite the divided but love : all else is a curse. Accursèd ! Accursèd be it to the aeons ! Hell.

42. Let it be that state of manyhood bound and loathing. So with thy all ; thou hast no right but to do thy will.

43. Do that, and no other shall say nay.

44. For pure will, unassuaged of purpose,

delivered from the lust of result, is every way perfect.

45.   The Perfect and the Perfect are one Perfect and not two ; nay, are none !

46.   Nothing is a secret key of this law. Sixty-one the Jews call it ; I call it eight, eighty, four hundred & eighteen.

47.   But they have the half : unite by thine art so that all disappear.

48.   My prophet is a fool with his one, one, one ; are not they the Ox, and none by the Book ?

49.   Abrogate are all rituals, all ordeals, all words and signs. Ra-Hoor-Khuit hath taken his seat in the East at the Equinox of the Gods ; and let Asar be with Isa, who also are one. But they are not of me. Let Asar be the adorant, Isa the sufferer ; Hoor in his secret name and splendour is the Lord initiating.

50.   There is a word to say about the Hiero-phantic task. Behold ! there are three ordeals in one, and it may be given in three ways. The gross must pass through fire ; let the fine be tried in intellect, and the lofty chosen ones in the highest. Thus ye have star & star, system & system ; let not one know well the other !

51.   There are four gates to one palace ; the

floor of that palace is of silver and gold ; lapis
lazuli & jasper are there ; and all rare scents ;
jasmine & rose, and the emblems of death. Let
him enter in turn or at once the four gates ; let
him stand on the floor of the palace. Will he not
sink ? Amn. Ho ! warrior, if thy servant sink ?
But there are means and means. Be goodly
therefore : dress ye all in fine apparel ; eat rich
foods and drink sweet wines and wines that foam !
Also, take your fill and will of love as ye will,
when, where and with whom ye will ! But always
unto me.

52. If this be not aright ; if ye confound the
space-marks, saying : They are one ; or saying,
They are many ; if the ritual be not ever unto me :
then expect the direful judgments of Ra Hoor
Khuit !

53. This shall regenerate the world, the little
world my sister, my heart & my tongue, unto
whom I send this kiss. Also, o scribe and prophet,
though thou be of the princes, it shall not assuage
thee nor absolve thee. But ecstasy be thine and
joy of earth : ever To me ! To me !

54. Change not as much as the style of a letter ;
for behold ! thou, o prophet, shalt not behold all
these mysteries hidden therein.

55. The child of thy bowels, *he* shall behold them.

56. Expect him not from the East, nor from the West; for from no expected house cometh that child. Aum! All words are sacred and all prophets true; save only that they understand a little; solve the first half of the equation, leave the second unattacked. But thou hast all in the clear light, and some, though not all, in the dark.

57. Invoke me under my stars! Love is the law, love under will. Nor let the fools mistake love; for there are love and love. There is the dove, and there is the serpent. Choose ye well! He, my prophet, hath chosen, knowing the law of the fortress, and the great mystery of the House of God.

All these old letters of my Book are aright; but ‫צ‬ is not the Star. This also is secret: my prophet shall reveal it to the wise.

58. I give unimaginable joys on earth: certainty, not faith, while in life, upon death; peace unutterable, rest, ecstasy; nor do I demand aught in sacrifice.

59. My incense is of resinous woods & gums; and there is no blood therein: because of my hair the trees of Eternity.

60.   My number is 11, as all their numbers who are of us.   The Five Pointed Star, with a Circle in the Middle, & the circle is Red.   My colour is black to the blind, but the blue & gold are seen of the seeing.   Also I have a secret glory for them that love me.

61.   But to love me is better than all things : if under the night-stars in the desert thou presently burnest mine incense before me, invoking me with a pure heart, and the Serpent flame therein, thou shalt come a little to lie in my bosom.   For one kiss wilt thou then be willing to give all ; but whoso gives one particle of dust shall lose all in that hour. Ye shall gather goods and store of women and spices ; ye shall wear rich jewels ; ye shall exceed the nations of the earth in splendour & pride ; but always in the love of me, and so shall ye come to my joy.   I charge you earnestly to come before me in a single robe, and covered with a rich headdress. I love you !   I yearn to you !   Pale or purple, veiled or voluptuous, I who am all pleasure and purple, and drunkenness of the innermost sense, desire you.   Put on the wings, and arouse the coiled splendour within you :   come unto me !

62.   At all my meetings with you shall the priestess say—and her eyes shall burn with desire

as she stands bare and rejoicing in my secret temple—To me ! To me ! calling forth the flame of the hearts of all in her love-chant.

63. Sing the rapturous love-song unto me ! Burn to me perfumes ! Wear to me jewels ! Drink to me, for I love you ! I love you !

64. I am the blue-lidded daughter of Sunset ; I am the naked brilliance of the voluptuous night-sky.

65. To me ! To me !

66. The Manifestation of Nuit is at an end.

1. Nu! the hiding of Hadit.
2. Come! all ye, and learn the secret that hath not yet been revealed. I, Hadit, am the complement of Nu, my bride. I am not extended, and Khabs is the name of my House.
3. In the sphere I am everywhere the centre, as she, the circumference, is nowhere found.
4. Yet she shall be known & I never.
5. Behold! the rituals of the old time are black. Let the evil ones be cast away; let the good ones be purged by the prophet! Then shall this Knowledge go aright.
6. I am the flame that burns in every heart of man, and in the core of every star. I am Life, and the giver of Life, yet therefore is the knowledge of me the knowledge of death.
7. I am the Magician and the Exorcist. I am the axle of the wheel, and the cube in the circle. " Come unto me " is a foolish word : for it is I that go.
8. Who worshipped Heru-pa-kraath have worshipped me; ill, for I am the worshipper.
9. Remember all ye that existence is pure joy; that all the sorrows are but as shadows; they pass & are done; but there is that which remains.

10. O prophet! thou hast ill will to learn this writing.

11. I see thee hate the hand & the pen; but I am stronger.

12. Because of me in Thee which thou knewest not.

13. for why? Because thou wast the knower, and me.

14. Now let there be a veiling of this shrine: now let the light devour men and eat them up with blindness!

15. For I am perfect, being Not; and my number is nine by the fools; but with the just I am eight, and one in eight: Which is vital, for I am none indeed. The Empress and the King are not of me; for there is a further secret.

16. I am The Empress & the Hierophant. Thus eleven, as my bride is eleven.

17. Hear me, ye people of sighing!
The sorrows of pain and regret
Are left to the dead and the dying,
The folk that not know me as yet.

18. These are dead, these fellows; they feel not. We are not for the poor and sad: the lords of the earth are our kinsfolk.

19. Is a God to live in a dog? No! but the

highest are of us. They shall rejoice, our chosen :
who sorroweth is not of us.

20. Beauty and strength, leaping laughter and
delicious languor, force and fire, are of us.

21. We have nothing with the outcast and the
unfit : let them die in their misery. For they feel
not. Compassion is the vice of kings : stamp down
the wretched & the weak : this is the law of the
strong : this is our law and the joy of the world.
Think not, o king, upon that lie : That Thou Must
Die : verily thou shalt not die, but live. Now let
it be understood : If the body of the King dissolve,
he shall remain in pure ecstasy for ever. Nuit !
Hadit ! Ra-Hoor-Khuit ! The Sun, Strength
& Sight, Light ; these are for the servants of
the Star & the Snake.

22. I am the Snake that giveth Knowledge
& Delight and bright glory, and stir the hearts of
men with drunkenness. To worship me take wine
and strange drugs whereof I will tell my prophet,
& be drunk thereof ! They shall not harm ye at
all. It is a lie, this folly against self. The exposure
of innocence is a lie. Be strong, o man ! lust,
enjoy all things of sense and rapture : fear not
that any God shall deny thee for this.

23. I am alone : there is no God where I am.

24. Behold! these be grave mysteries; for there are also of my friends who be hermits. Now think not to find them in the forest or on the mountain; but in beds of purple, caressed by magnificent beasts of women with large limbs, and fire and light in their eyes, and masses of flaming hair about them; there shall ye find them. Ye shall see them at rule, at victorious armies, at all the joy; and there shall be in them a joy a million times greater than this. Beware lest any force another, King against King! Love one another with burning hearts; on the low men trample in the fierce lust of your pride, in the day of your wrath.

25. Ye are against the people, O my chosen!

26. I am the secret Serpent coiled about to spring: in my coiling there is joy. If I lift up my head, I and my Nuit are one. If I droop down mine head, and shoot forth venom, then is rapture of the earth, and I and the earth are one.

27. There is great danger in me; for who doth not understand these runes shall make a great miss. He shall fall down into the pit called Because, and there he shall perish with the dogs of Reason.

28. Now a curse upon Because and his kin!

29.   May Because be accursèd for ever!

30.   If Will stops and cries Why, invoking Because, then Will stops & does nought.

31.   If Power asks why, then is Power weakness.

32.   Also reason is a lie; for there is a factor infinite & unknown; & all their words are skew-wise.

33.   Enough of Because! Be he damned for a dog!

34.   But ye, o my people, rise up & awake!

35.   Let the rituals be rightly performed with joy & beauty!

36.   There are rituals of the elements and feasts of the times.

37.   A feast for the first night of the Prophet and his Bride!

38.   A feast for the three days of the writing of the Book of the Law.

39.   A feast for Tahuti and the child of the Prophet—secret, O Prophet!

40.   A feast for the Supreme Ritual, and a feast for the Equinox of the Gods.

41.   A feast for fire and a feast for water; a feast for life and a greater feast for death!

42.   A feast every day in your hearts in the joy of my rapture!

43. A feast every night unto Nu, and the pleasure of uttermost delight!

44. Aye! feast! rejoice! there is no dread hereafter. There is the dissolution, and eternal ecstasy in the kisses of Nu.

45. There is death for the dogs.

46. Dost thou fail? Art thou sorry? Is fear in thine heart?

47. Where I am these are not.

48. Pity not the fallen! I never knew them. I am not for them. I console not: I hate the consoled & the consoler.

49. I am unique & conqueror. I am not of the slaves that perish. Be they damned & dead! Amen. (This is of the 4: there is a fifth who is invisible, & therein am I as a babe in an egg.)

50. Blue am I and gold in the light of my bride: but the red gleam is in my eyes; & my spangles are purple & green.

51. Purple beyond purple: it is the light higher than eyesight.

52. There is a veil: that veil is black. It is the veil of the modest woman; it is the veil of sorrow, & the pall of death: this is none of me. Tear down that lying spectre of the centuries: veil not your vices in virtuous words: these vices

are my service; ye do well, & I will reward you here and hereafter.

53. Fear not, o prophet, when these words are said, thou shalt not be sorry. Thou art emphatically my chosen; and blessed are the eyes that thou shalt look upon with gladness. But I will hide thee in a mask of sorrow: they that see thee shall fear thou art fallen: but I lift thee up.

54. Nor shall they who cry aloud their folly that thou meanest nought avail; thou shall reveal it: thou availest: they are the slaves of because: They are not of me. The stops as thou wilt; the letters? change them not in style or value!

55. Thou shalt obtain the order & value of the English Alphabet; thou shalt find new symbols to attribute them unto.

56. Begone! ye mockers; even though ye laugh in my honour ye shall laugh not long: then when ye are sad know that I have forsaken you.

57. He that is righteous shall be righteous still; he that is filthy shall be filthy still.

58. Yea! deem not of change: ye shall be as ye are, & not other. Therefore the kings

of the earth shall be Kings for ever : the slaves shall serve. There is none that shall be cast down or lifted up : all is ever as it was. Yet there are masked ones my servants : it may be that yonder beggar is a King. A King may choose his garment as he will : there is no certain test : but a beggar cannot hide his poverty.

59. Beware therefore ! Love all, lest perchance is a King concealed ! Say you so ? Fool ! If he be a King, thou canst not hurt him.

60. Therefore strike hard & low, and to hell with them, master !

61. There is a light before thine eyes, o prophet, a light undesired, most desirable.

62. I am uplifted in thine heart ; and the kisses of the stars rain hard upon thy body.

63. Thou art exhaust in the voluptuous fullness of the inspiration ; the expiration is sweeter than death, more rapid and laughterful than a caress of Hell's own worm.

64. Oh ! thou art overcome : we are upon thee ; our delight is all over thee : hail ! hail : prophet of Nu ! prophet of Had ! prophet of Ra-Hoor-Khu ! Now rejoice ! now come in our splendour & rapture ! Come in our passionate peace, & write sweet words for the Kings !

65. I am the Master: thou art the Holy Chosen One.

66. Write, & find ecstasy in writing! Work, & be our bed in working! Thrill with the joy of life & death! Ah! thy death shall be lovely: whoso seeth it shall be glad. Thy death shall be the seal of the promise of our agelong love. Come! lift up thine heart & rejoice! We are one; we are none.

67. Hold! Hold! Bear up in thy rapture; fall not in swoon of the excellent kisses!

68. Harder! Hold up thyself! Lift thine head! breathe not so deep—die!

69. Ah! Ah! What do I feel? Is the word exhausted?

70. There is help & hope in other spells. Wisdom says: be strong! Then canst thou bear more joy. Be not animal; refine thy rapture! If thou drink, drink by the eight and ninety rules of art: if thou love, exceed by delicacy; and if thou do aught joyous, let there be subtlety therein!

71. But exceed! exceed!

72. Strive ever to more! and if thou art truly mine—and doubt it not, an if thou art ever joyous!—death is the crown of all.

73. Ah! Ah! Death! Death! thou shalt

long for death. Death is forbidden, o man, unto thee.

74. The length of thy longing shall be the strength of its glory. He that lives long & desires death much is ever the King among the Kings.

75. Aye! listen to the numbers & the words:

76. 4 6 3 8 A B K 2 4 A L G M O R 3 Y X 24 89 R P S T O V A L. What meaneth this, o prophet? Thou knowest not; nor shalt thou know ever. There cometh one to follow thee: he shall expound it. But remember, o chosen one, to be me; to follow the love of Nu in the star-lit heaven; to look forth upon men, to tell them this glad word.

77. O be thou proud and mighty among men!

78. Lift up thyself! for there is none like unto thee among men or among Gods! Lift up thyself, o my prophet, thy stature shall surpass the stars. They shall worship thy name, foursquare, mystic, wonderful, the number of the man; and the name of thy house 418.

79. The end of the hiding of Hadit; and blessing & worship to the prophet of the lovely Star!

1. Abrahadabra; the reward of Ra Hoor Khut.

2. There is division hither homeward; there is a word not known. Spelling is defunct; all is not aught. Beware! Hold! Raise the spell of Ra-Hoor-Khuit!

3. Now let it be first understood that I am a god of War and of Vengeance. I shall deal hardly with them.

4. Choose ye an island!

5. Fortify it!

6. Dung it about with enginery of war!

7. I will give you a war-engine.

8. With it ye shall smite the peoples; and none shall stand before you.

9. Lurk! Withdraw! Upon them! this is the Law of the Battle of Conquest: thus shall my worship be about my secret house.

10. Get the stélé of revealing itself; set it in thy secret temple—and that temple is already aright disposed—& it shall be your Kiblah for ever. It shall not fade, but miraculous colour shall come back to it day after day. Close it in locked glass for a proof to the world.

11. This shall be your only proof. I forbid argument. Conquer! That is enough. I will

make easy to you the abstruction from the ill-ordered house in the Victorious City. Thou shalt thyself convey it with worship, o prophet, though thou likest it not. Thou shalt have danger & trouble. Ra-Hoor-Khu is with thee. Worship me with fire & blood; worship me with swords & with spears. Let the woman be girt with a sword before me : let blood flow to my name. Trample down the Heathen; be upon them, o warrior, I will give you of their flesh to eat!

12. Sacrifice cattle, little and big : after a child.

13. But not now.

14. Ye shall see that hour, o blessèd Beast, and thou the Scarlet Concubine of his desire!

15. Ye shall be sad thereof.

16. Deem not too eagerly to catch the promises ; fear not to undergo the curses. Ye, even ye, know not this meaning all.

17. Fear not at all ; fear neither men nor Fates, nor gods, nor anything. Money fear not, nor laughter of the folk folly, nor any other power in heaven or upon the earth or under the earth. Nu is your refuge as Hadit your light ; and I am the strength, force, vigour, of your arms.

18. Mercy let be off : damn them who pity ! Kill and torture ; spare not ; be upon them !

19. That stélé they shall call the Abomination of Desolation ; count well its name, & it shall be to you as 718.

20. Why ? Because of the fall of Because, that he is not there again.

21. Set up my image in the East : thou shalt buy thee an image which I will show thee, especial, not unlike the one thou knowest. And it shall be suddenly easy for thee to do this.

22. The other images group around me to support me : let all be worshipped, for they shall cluster to exalt me. I am the visible object of worship ; the others are secret ; for the Beast & his Bride are they : and for the winners of the Ordeal x. What is this ? Thou shalt know.

23. For perfume mix meal & honey & thick leavings of red wine : then oil of Abramelin and olive oil, and afterward soften & smooth down with rich fresh blood.

24. The best blood is of the moon, monthly : then the fresh blood of a child, or dropping from the host of heaven : then of enemies ; then of the priest or of the worshippers : last of some beast, no matter what.

25. This burn : of this make cakes & eat unto me. This hath also another use ; let it be laid before me, and kept thick with perfumes of your orison : it shall become full of beetles as it were and creeping things sacred unto me.

26. These slay, naming your enemies ; & they shall fall before you.

27. Also these shall breed lust & power of lust in you at the eating thereof.

28. Also ye shall be strong in war.

29. Moreover, be they long kept, it is better ; for they swell with my force. All before me.

30. My altar is of open brass work : burn thereon in silver or gold !

31. There cometh a rich man from the West who shall pour his gold upon thee.

32. From gold forge steel !

33. Be ready to fly or to smite !

34. But your holy place shall be untouched throughout the centuries : though with fire and sword it be burnt down & shattered, yet an invisible house there standeth, and shall stand until the fall of the Great Equinox ; when Hrumachis shall arise and the double-wanded one assume my throne and place. Another prophet shall arise, and bring fresh fever from

the skies ; another woman shall awake the lust
& worship of the Snake ; another soul of God and
beast shall mingle in the globèd priest ; another
sacrifice shall stain the tomb ; another king shall
reign ; and blessing no longer be poured To the
Hawk-headed mystical Lord !

35.   The half of the word of Heru-ra-ha, called
Hoor-pa-kraat and Ra-Hoor-Khut.

36.   Then said the prophet unto the God :

37.   I adore thee in the song—

I am the Lord of Thebes, and I
    The inspired forth-speaker of Mentu ;
For me unveils the veilèd sky,
    The self-slain Ankh-af-na-khonsu
Whose words are truth. I invoke, I greet
    Thy presence, O Ra-Hoor-Khuit !

Unity uttermost showed !
    I adore the might of Thy breath,
Supreme and terrible God,
    Who makest the gods and death
To tremble before Thee :—
    I, I adore thee !

Appear on the throne of Ra !
Open the ways of the Khu !
Lighten the ways of the Ka !
The ways of the Khabs run through
To stir me or still me !
Aum ! let it fill me !

38.   So that thy light is in me ; & its red flame
is as a sword in my hand to push thy order.   There
is a secret door that I shall make to establish thy
way in all the quarters, (these are the adorations,
as thou hast written), as it is said :

The light is mine ; its rays consume
Me : I have made a secret door
Into the House of Ra and Tum,
Of Khephra and of Ahathoor.
I am thy Theban, O Mentu,
The prophet Ankh-af-na-khonsu !

By Bes-na-Maut my breast I beat ;
By wise Ta-Nech I weave my spell.
Show thy star-splendour, O Nuit !
Bid me within thine House to dwell,
O wingèd snake of light, Hadit !
Abide with me, Ra-Hoor-Khuit !

39. All this and a book to say how thou didst come hither and a reproduction of this ink and paper for ever—for in it is the word secret & not only in the English—and thy comment upon this the Book of the Law shall be printed beautifully in red ink and black upon beautiful paper made by hand ; and to each man and woman that thou meetest, were it but to dine or to drink at them, it is the Law to give. Then they shall chance to abide in this bliss or no ; it is no odds. Do this quickly !

40. But the work of the comment ? That is easy ; and Hadit burning in thy heart shall make swift and secure thy pen.

41. Establish at thy Kaaba a clerk-house : all must be done well and with business way.

42. The ordeals thou shalt oversee thyself, save only the blind ones. Refuse none, but thou shalt know & destroy the traitors. I am Ra-Hoor-Khuit ; and I am powerful to protect my servant. Success is thy proof : argue not ; convert not ; talk not overmuch ! Them that seek to entrap thee, to overthrow thee, them attack without pity or quarter ; & destroy them utterly. Swift as a trodden serpent turn and strike ! Be thou yet deadlier than he ! Drag down their souls

to awful torment : laugh at their fear : spit upon them !

43. Let the Scarlet Woman beware ! If pity and compassion and tenderness visit her heart ; if she leave my work to toy with old sweetnesses ; then shall my vengeance be known. I will slay me her child : I will alienate her heart : I will cast her out from men : as a shrinking and despised harlot shall she crawl through dusk wet streets, and die cold and an-hungered.

44. But let her raise herself in pride ! Let her follow me in my way ! Let her work the work of wickedness ! Let her kill her heart ! Let her be loud and adulterous ! Let her be covered with jewels, and rich garments, and let her be shameless before all men !

45. Then will I lift her to pinnacles of power : then will I breed from her a child mightier than all the kings of the earth. I will fill her with joy : with my force shall she see & strike at the worship of Nu : she shall achieve Hadit.

46. I am the warrior Lord of the Forties : the Eighties cower before me, & are abased. I will bring you to victory & joy : I will be at your arms in battle & ye shall delight to slay. Success is your proof ; courage is your armour ; go on, go on,

in my strength ; & ye shall turn not back for any !

47.   This book shall be translated into all tongues : but always with the original in the writing of the Beast ; for in the chance shape of the letters and their position to one another : in these are mysteries that no Beast shall divine. Let him not seek to try : but one cometh after him, whence I say not, who shall discover the Key of it all.   Then this line drawn is a key : then this circle squared in its failure is a key also.   And Abrahadabra.   It shall be his child & that strangely. Let him not seek after this ; for thereby alone can he fall from it.

48.   Now this mystery of the letters is done, and I want to go on to the holier place.

49.   I am in a secret fourfold word, the blasphemy against all gods of men.

50.   Curse them ! Curse them ! Curse them !

51.   With my Hawk's head I peck at the eyes of Jesus as he hangs upon the cross.

52.   I flap my wings in the face of Mohammed & blind him.

53.   With my claws I tear out the flesh of the Indian and the Buddhist, Mongol and Din.

54.   Bahlasti ! Ompehda !   I spit on your crapulous creeds.

55. Let Mary inviolate be torn upon wheels : for her sake let all chaste women be utterly despised among you !

56. Also for beauty's sake and love's !

57. Despise also all cowards ; professional soldiers who dare not fight, but play ; all fools despise !

58. But the keen and the proud, the royal and the lofty ; ye are brothers !

59. As brothers fight ye !

60. There is no law beyond Do what thou wilt.

61. There is an end of the word of the God enthroned in Ra's seat, lightening the girders of the soul.

62. To Me do ye reverence ! to me come ye through tribulation of ordeal, which is bliss.

63. The fool readeth this Book of the Law, and its comment ; & he understandeth it not.

64. Let him come through the first ordeal, & it will be to him as silver.

65. Through the second, gold.

66. Through the third, stones of precious water.

67. Through the fourth, ultimate sparks of the intimate fire.

68. Yet to all it shall seem beautiful. Its enemies who say not so, are mere liars.

69.   There is success.

70.   I am the Hawk-Headed Lord of Silence & of Strength ; my nemyss shrouds the night-blue sky.

71.   Hail ! ye twin warriors about the pillars of the world ! for your time is nigh at hand.

72.   I am the Lord of the Double Wand of Power ; the wand of the Force of Coph Nia—but my left hand is empty, for I have crushed an Universe ; & nought remains.

73.   Paste the sheets from right to left and from top to bottom : then behold !

74.   There is a splendour in my name hidden and glorious, as the sun of midnight is ever the son.

75.   The ending of the words is the Word Abrahadabra.

The Book of the Law is Written
and Concealed.
Aum.   Ha.

THE COMMENT.

Do what thou wilt shall be the whole of the Law.

The study of this Book is forbidden. It is wise to destroy this copy after the first reading.

Whosoever disregards this does so at his own risk and peril. These are most dire.

Those who discuss the contents of this Book are to be shunned by all, as centres of pestilence.

All questions of the Law are to be decided only by appeal to my writings, each for himself.

There is no law beyond Do what thou wilt.

Love is the law, love under will.

The priest of the princes,

ANKH-F-N-KHONSU

THE FACSIMILE

OF THE ORIGINAL

HANDWRITTEN

MANUSCRIPT

OF LIBER

AL

Had! The manifestation of Nuit

The unveiling of the company of heaven

Every man and every woman is a star

Every number is infinite; there is no difference

Help me, o warrior lord of Thebes, in my unveiling before the children of men

Be thou Hadit, my secret centre, my heart & my tongue.

Behold! it is revealed by Aiwass the minister of Hoor-paar-kraat

The Khabs is in the Khu, not the Khu in the Khabs

Worship then the Khabs, and behold my light shed over you.

2

Let my servants be few & secret : they shall
rule the many & the known.

These are fools that men adore ; both their
Gods & their men are fools.

Come forth, o children, under the stars
& take your fill of love . I am above you
and in you . My ecstasy is in yours. My
joy is to see your joy

V. 1. of Spell called the Sky.

Now ye shall know that The chosen
priest & apostle of infinite space is
the prince-priest the Beast and in

his woman; called The Scarlet Woman, is all power given. They shall gather my children into their fold : they shall bring the glory of the stars into the hearts of men.

For he is ever a sun, and she a moon. But to him is the winged secret flame and to her the stooping starlight.

But ye are not so chosen

Burn upon their brows, o splendrous serpent!

O azure-lidded woman, bend upon them!

The key of the rituals is in the secret word which I have given unto him

With the God & the Adorer I am nothing : they
do not see me . They are as upon the earth
I am Heaven, and there is no other God
than me, and my lord Hadit.

Now therefore I am known to ye by my
name Nuit, and to him by a secret name
which I will give him when at last he
knoweth me

Since I am Infinite Space and the Infinite
Stars thereof, do ye also thus. Bind
nothing ! Let there be no difference made
among you between any one thing & any

other thing; for thereby there cometh hurt.

But whoso availeth in this, let him be
the chief of all!

I am Nuit, and my word is six and fifty.

Divide, add, multiply and understand.

Then saith the prophet and slave of the
beauteous one : Who am I, and what shall
be the sign. So she answered him, bending
down, a lambent flame of blue, all-touching,
all penetrant, her lovely hands upon the
black earth, & her lithe body arched for love,
and her soft feet not hurting the

6

little flowers Thou knowest! And the sigh

shall be my ecstasy, the consciousness of

the continuity of existence, ~~the~~ the ~~not~~

omnipresence of my body, ~~the~~ ~~affirm fact of my immortality~~

(~~Write this in whiter words~~) | One letter as
                                                    above.

(But go ~~forth on~~)

Then He put forward & said unto

the Queen of Space, kissing her lovely brows

and the dew of her light bathing his whole

body in a sweet-smelling perfume of Sweat

O Nuit, continuous one of Heaven, let it

be ever thus, that men speak not of
Thee as One but as None and let
them speak not of thee at all since
thou art continuous.

None, breathed the light, faint & faery, of
the stars, and two. For I am divided
for love's sake, for the chance of union.
This is the creation of the world, that
the pain of ~~division~~ division is as nothing and
the joy of dissolution all.
For these fools of men and their

8

woes are not Thou at all! They feel
little; what is, is balanced by weak
joys: but ye are my chosen ones.

Obey my prophet! follow out the
ordeals of my knowledge! seek me
only! Then the joys of my love will
redeem ye from all pain. This is
so: I swear it by the vault of my
body; by my sacred heart and tongue;
by all I can give, by all I desire of
ye all.
Then the priest fell into a deep trance or

9

swoon & said unto the Queen of Heaven

Write unto us the ordeals write unto
us the rituals write unto us the law.

But she said the ordeals I write not
the rituals shall be half known and
half concealed: the Law is for all

This that thou writest is the threefold
book of Law

My scribe Ankh-af-na-khonsu the
priest of the princes shall not in one
letter change this book; but lest there
be folly, he shall comment thereupon
by the wisdom of Ra-Hoor-Khu-it.

Also the mantras and spells; the
obeah and the wanga; the work of
the wand and the work of the
sword: these he shall learn and teach.
He must teach; but he may make severe
the ordeals.

The word of the Law is Θελημα.

Who calls us Thelemites will do no
wrong, if he look but close into the
word. For there are three
Grades, the Hermit and the Lover and
the man of ~~Earth~~. Do what thou wilt

shall be the whole of the Law.

The word of Sin is Restriction. O man!
refuse not thy wife if she will. O
lover, if thou wilt, depart. There is
no bond that can unite the divided but
love: all else is a curse. Accursèd!
Accursèd! be it to the aeons. Hell.
Let it be that state of manyhood
bound and loathing. So with thy all
thou hast no right but to do thy will
Do that, and no other shall say nay
For pure will, unassuaged of purpose,

delivered from the lust of result, is
every way perfect—

The Perfect and the Perfect are one
Perfect and not two; nay, are none!

Nothing is a secret key of this law

Sixty-one the Jews call it; I call it
Eight, eighty, four hundred & eighteen.

But they have the half: unite by thine
art so that all disappear.

My prophet is a fool with his one one
one; are not they the Ox and none
by the Book.

Abrogate are all rituals, all ordeals all
words and signs. Ra-Hoor-Khuit hath
taken his seat in the east at the Equinox
of the Gods and let Asar be with Isa
who also are one. But they are not of
me. Let Asar be the adorant, Isa the
sufferer; Hoor in his secret name and
splendour is the Lord initiating.

There is a word to say about the Hierophantic
task. Behold! there are three ordeals in
one, and it may be given in three ways.
The gross must pass through fire; let the

fine be tried in intellect, and the
lofty whose & ones in the high test. Thus
ye have star & star system & system
let not one know well the other.

There are four gates to one palace;
the floor of that place is of silver and
gold, lapis lazuli & jasper are there, and
all rare scents jasmine & rose, and the
emblems of death. Let him enter in then
or at once the four gates; let him stand
on the floor of the palace. Will he
not drink? Ann. Ho! warrior, if thy
servant drink? But there are means

and means. Be goodly therefore: dress ye
all in fine apparel eat rich foods and
drink sweet wines and wines that foam.
~~bast~~ Also, take your fill and will of
love as ye will, when, where and with
whom ye will. But always unto me.
If this be not aright; if ye confound
the space-marks, saying: They are one
or saying They are many; if the ritual
be not ever unto me: then expect
the dreadful judgments of Ra Hoor Khuit
This shall regenerate the world, the little

world my sister, my heart & my tongue, unto whom I send this kiss. Also, o scribe and prophet—though thou be of the princes it shall not assuage thee nor absolve thee. But ecstasy be thine and joy of earth: ever To me To me

Change not as much as the style of a letter; for behold thou o prophet shalt not behold all these mysteries hidden therein.

The child of thy bowels, he shall behold them.

Expect him not from the East nor from

the West; for from no expected house cometh that child. Aum! All words are sacred and all prophets true; save only that they understand a little; solve the first half of the equation, leave the second unattacked. But thou hast all in the clear light, and some, though not all, in the dark.

Invoke me under my stars. Love is the law, love under will. Nor let the fools mistake love; for there are love and love. There is the dove and there is the serpent. Choose ye well! He, my prophet, hath

Chosen, knowing the law of the fortress and the great mystery of the House of God

All these old letters of my Book are aright; but [Tzaddi] is not the Star. This also is secret: my prophet shall reveal it to the wise.

I give unimaginable joys on earth: certainty, not faith, while in life, upon death; peace unutterable, rest, ecstasy: nor do I demand aught in sacrifice.

My incense is of resinous woods & gums and there is no blood therein: because of my hair the trees of Eternity.

My number is 11, as all their numbers who are of us. (Lost) (Heaven?) My colour is black to the blind, but the blue & gold are seen of the seeing. The shape of my star is The two-pointed star, with a circle in the middle, & the circle is Red. Also I have a secret glory for them that love me.

But to love me is better than all things: if under the night-stars in the desert thou presently burnest mine incense before me, invoking me with a pure heart, and the Serpent flame therein, then shalt thou come a little to lie in my bosom. For one kiss wilt thou then be willing to give all:

but whoso gives one particle of dust shall lose all in that hour. Ye shall gather goods and store of women and spices; ye shall wear rich jewels; ye shall exceed the nations of the earth in splendour & pride; but always in the love of me, and so shall ye come to my joy. I charge you earnestly to come before me in a single robe and crowned with a rich headdress. I love you! I yearn to you. Pale or purple, veiled or voluptuous, I who am all pleasure and purple

and drunkenness of the innermost sense
desire you. Put on the wings and arouse
the coiled splendour within you: come unto me
At all my meetings with you shall the
priestess say — and her eyes shall burn
with desire as she stands bare and rejoicing
in my secret temple — To me! To me!
calling forth the flame of the hearts of all in her
love — chant.
Sing the rapturous love-song unto me!
Burn to me perfumes! Wear to me jewels!
Drink to me, for I love you! I love you!

I am the blue-lidded daughter of sunset; I am the naked brilliance of the voluptuous night sky

To me! To me!

The Manifestation of Nuit is at an End.

Nu! the hiding of Hadit.

2 Come! all ye, and learn the secret that hath not yet been revealed. I, Hadit am the complement of Nu my bride. I am not extended, and Khabs is the name of my House.

3 In the Sphere I am everywhere, the centre, as She, the circumference, is nowhere found.

4 Yet she shall be known & I never.

5 Behold! the rituals of the old time are black. Let the evil ones be cast away; let the good ones be purged by the prophet! Then shall this Knowledge go aright.

6. I am the flame that burns in every heart of man, and in the core of every star. I am

Life, and the giver of Life; yet therefore is the knowledge of me the knowledge of death.

7. I am the Magician and the Exorcist. I am the axle of the wheel, and the cube in the circle. "Come unto me" is a foolish word; for it is I that go.

8 Who worshipped Heru-pa-kraath have worshipped me; ill, for I am the worshipper.

9 Remember all ye that existence is pure joy; that all the sorrows are but as shadows; they pass & are done; but there is that which remains.

10. O prophet! thou hast ill will to learn this writing.

11. I see thee hate the hand & the pen: but I am

12 Because of me in Thee which Thou knewest not.

13. For why? Because thou wast the knower, and me.

14. Now let there be a veiling of this shrine: now let the light devour men and eat them up with blindness.

15. For I am perfect, being Not; and my number is nine by the fools; but with the just I am Eight, and one in eight: Which is vital, for I am none indeed. The Empress and the King are not of me; for there is a further secret.

16 I am the Empress and the Hierophant. Thus eleven as my bride is eleven.

17) Hear me, ye people of sighing!

    The sorrows of pain and regret
Are left to the dead and the dying,
    The folk that not know me as yet.

18 These are dead, these fellows; they feel not. We are not for the poor and sad: the lords of the earth are our kinsfolk.

19 Is a God to live in a dog? No! but the highest are of us. They shall rejoice, our chosen: who sorroweth is not of us.

20 Beauty and strength, leaping laughter and delicious languor, force and fire, are of us.

We have nothing with the outcast and the unfit: let them die in their misery. For they feel not. Compassion is the vice of kings: stamp down the wretched & the weak: this is the law of the strong: this is our law and the joy of the world. Think not, o king, upon that lie: That Thou Must Die: verily thou shalt not die, but live! Now let it be understood: If the body of the King dissolve, he shall remain in pure ecstasy for ever. Nuit! Hadit! Ra-Hoor-Khuit! The Sun, Strength & Sight, Light; these are for the servants of the Star & the Snake

22 I am the Snake that giveth Knowledge & Delight and bright glory, and stir the hearts of men with drunkenness. To worship me take wine and strange drugs whereof I will tell my prophet, & be drunk thereof! They shall not harm ye at all. It is a lie, this folly against self. The exposure of innocence is a lie. Be strong, o man, lust, enjoy all things of sense and rapture: fear not that any God shall deny thee for this.

23 I am alone: there is no God where I am.

24 Behold! these be grave mysteries; for there are also of my friends who be hermits. Now

Think not to find them in the forest or on the mountain; but in beds of purple, caressed by magnificent beasts of women with large limbs, and fire and light in their eyes, and masses of flaming hair about them; there shall ye find them. Ye shall see them at rule, at victorious armies, at all the joy; and there shall be in them a joy a million times greater than this. Beware lest any force another, King against King! Love one another with burning hearts; or the low men trample in the fierce lust of your pride in the day of your wrath.

25. Ye are against the people, O my chosen!

26. I am the secret Serpent coiled about to spring: in my coiling there is joy. If I lift up my head, I and my Nuit are one. If I droop down mine head, and shoot forth venom, then is rapture of the earth, and I and the earth are one.

27. There is great danger in me; for who doth not understand these runes shall make a great **miss**. He shall fall down into the pit called Because, and there he shall

...ion with the dogs of Reason.

28 Now a curse upon Because and his kin!

29 May Because be accursèd for ever!

30 If Will stops and cries Why, invoking Because, then Will stops & does nought.

31 If Power asks why, then is Power weakness.

32 Also reason is a lie; for there is a factor infinite & unknown; & all their words are skew-wise.

33 Enough of Because! Be he damned for a dog!

34. But ye, o my people, rise up & awake!

35. Let the rituals be rightly performed with joy & beauty!

36 There are rituals of the elements and feasts of the times.

37 A feast for the first night of the Prophet and his Bride!

38 A feast for the three days of the writing of the Book of the Law.

39 A feast for Tahuti and the child of the Prophet — secret, O Prophet!

40 A feast for the Supreme Ritual, and a feast for the Equinox of the Gods.

41 A feast for fire and a feast for water; a feast for life and a greater feast for death!

42 A feast every day in your hearts in the joy of my rapture.

43 A feast every night unto Nu, and the pleasure of uttermost delight.

44 Aye! feast! rejoice! there is no dread hereafter. There is the dissolution, and eternal ecstasy in the kisses of Nu.

45 There is death for the dogs.

46 Dost thou fail? Art thou sorry? Is fear in thine heart?

47 Where I am these are not.

48 Pity not the fallen! I never knew them.
I am not for them. I console not. I hate
the consoled & the consoler.

49 I am unique & conqueror. I am not of the
slaves that perish. Be they damned &
dead! Amen. [This is of the 4: there is
a fifth who is invisible & therein am I
as a babe in an egg.]

50 Blue am I and gold in the light of my
bride: but the red gleam is in my eyes
& my spangles are purple & green.

51. Purple beyond purple: it is the light higher

than eyesight.

52 There is a veil: that veil is black. It is
the veil of the modest woman; it is the veil
of sorrow, & the pall of death: this is none
of me. Tear down that lying spectre of
the centuries: veil not your vices in
virtuous words: these vices are my service:
ye do well, & I will reward you here and
hereafter.

53 Fear not, O prophet, when these words are
said, thou shalt not be sorry. Thou art
emphatically my chosen; and blessed are

the eyes that thou shalt look upon with gladness. But I will hide thee in a mask of sorrow: they that see thee shall fear thou art fallen: but I lift thee up.

54 Nor shall they who cry aloud their folly that thou meanest nought avail; thou shalt reveal it: thou availest: they are the slaves of because: They are not of me. The stops as thou wilt; the letters change them not in style or value!

55 Thou shalt obtain the order & value of the English Alphabet; thou shalt find

new symbols to attribute them unto.

56. Begone! ye mockers; even though ye laugh in my honour ye shall laugh not long: then when ye are sad know that I have forsaken you.

57. He that is righteous shall be righteous still; he that is filthy shall be filthy still.

58 Yea! deem not of change: ye shall be as ye are, & not other. Therefore the kings of the earth shall be Kings for ever: the slaves shall serve. There is none that shall be cast down or lifted up: all is ever

as it was. Yet there are masked men, my servants: it may be that yonder beggar is a King. A King may choose his garment as he will: there is no certain test: but a beggar cannot hide his poverty.

59 Beware therefore! Love all, lest perchance is a King concealed! Say you so? Fool! If he be a King, thou canst not hurt him.

60 Therefore strike hard & low, and to hell with them, master!

61 There is a light before thine eyes of prophet a light undesired, most desirable.

62 I am uplifted in thine heart and the kisses
   of the stars rain hard upon thy body..

63 Thou art exhaust in the voluptuous fullness
   of the aspiration: the aspiration is sweeter
   than death, more rapid and laughterful than
   a caress of Hell's own worm.

64 O! thou art overcome: we are upon thee;
   our delight is all over thee: hail! hail!
   prophet of Nu! prophet of Had! prophet of
   Ra - Hoor Khu! Now rejoice! now come in
   our splendour & rapture! Come in our passionate
   peace, & write sweet words for the Kings!

65 I am the Master: thou art the Holy Chosen One,

66 Write, & find ecstasy in writing! Work & be our bed in working! Thrill with the joy of life & death! Ah! thy death shall be lovely: whoso seeth it shall be glad. Thy death shall be the seal of the promise of our agelong love. Come! lift up thine heart & rejoice! We are one; we are none.

67 Hold! Hold! Bear up in thy rapture; fall not in swoon of the excellent kisses!

68 Harder! Hold up thyself! Lift thine head!

breathe not so deep — die!

69 Ah! Ah! What dost feel? Is the word Exhausted?

70 There is help & hope in other spells. Wisdom says: be strong! Then canst thou bear more joy. Be not animal; refine thy rapture! If thou drink, drink by the eight and ninety rules of art: if thou love, exceed by delicacy; and if thou do aught joyous, let there be subtlety therein!

71 But exceed! exceed!

72 Strive ever to more! and if thou art truly

mine. — and doubt it not, an if thou art ever joyous! — death is the crown of all

33 Ah! Ah! Death! Death! thou shalt long for death. Death is forbidden, o man, unto thee.

74 The length of thy longing shall be the strength of its glory. He that lives long & desires death much is ever the King among the Kings.

75 Aye! listen to the numbers & the words:

76   4638 A B K 2 4 A L G M O R 3 Y
   × 24 89 R P S T O V A L. What meaneth this, o prophet? Thou knowest not; nor shalt thou know ever. There cometh one to follow thee: he shall

Expound it. But remember, o Chosen one, to be me; to follow the love of Nu in the star-lit heaven; to look forth upon men, to tell them this glad word.

37 O be thou proud and mighty among men!

38 Lift up thyself! for there is none like unto thee among men or among Gods! Lift up thyself, o my prophet, thy stature shall surpass the stars. They shall worship thy name, foursquare, mystic, wonderful, the number of the man; and the name of

My house 418.

79 The end of the building of Judith; and
blessing and worship to the prophet of
the lovely Star.

1 Abrahadabra! the reward of Ra Hoor Khut.

2 There is division hither homeward; there is a word not known. Spelling is defunct; all is not aught. Beware! Hold! Raise the spell of Ra-Hoor-Khuit.

3 Now let it be first understood that I am a god of War and of Vengeance. I shall deal hardly with them.

4 Choose ye an island!

5 Fortify it!

6 Dung it about with enginery of war!

7 I will give you a war-engine.

8 With it ye shall smite the peoples and

none shall stand before you.

9 Lurk! Withdraw! Upon them! This
is The Law of the Battle of Conquest: thus
shall my worship be about my secret house.

10 Get the stélé of revealing itself; set it
in thy secret temple — and that temple
is already aright disposed — & it shall be your
Kiblah for ever. It shall not fade, but
miraculous colour shall come back to it
day after day. Close it in locked glass for a
proof to the world.

11 This shall be your only proof. I forbid argument.
Conquer! That is enough. I will make easy

to you the abstraction from the ill-ordered house in the Victorious City. Thou shalt thyself convey it with worship, o prophet, though thou likest it not. Thou shalt have danger & trouble. Ra-Hoor-Khu is with thee. Worship me with fire & blood; worship me with swords & with spears. Let the woman be girt with a sword before me: let blood flow to my name. Trample down the Heathen; be upon them, o warrior, I will give you of their flesh to eat!

12 Sacrifice cattle little and big: after a child.

13 But not now.

14 Ye shall see that hour, o blessèd Beast, and thou the Scarlet Concubine of his desire!

15 Ye shall be sad thereof.

16 Seem not too eagerly to catch the promises; seem not to undergo the curses. Ye, even ye, know not this meaning all.

17 Fear not at all; fear neither men, nor Fates, nor gods, nor anything. Money fear not, nor laughter of the folk folly, nor any other power in heaven or upon the earth or under the earth. Nu is your refuge as Hadit your

5

light; and I am the strength, force, vigour, of
your arms.

18 Mercy let be off: damn them who pity.
Kill and torture; spare not; be upon them.

19 That stélé they shall call the Abomination
of Desolation; count well its name, & it shall
be to you as 718.

20 Why? Because of the fall of Because, that
he is not there again.

21 Set up my image in the East: thou shalt buy
thee an image which I will show thee, especially
not unlike the one thou knowest. And it shall
be suddenly easy for thee to do this.

22. The other images group around me to support me: let all be worshipped, for they shall cluster to exalt me. I am the visible object of worship; the others are secret; for the Beast & his Bride are they: and for the winners of the Ordeal x. What is this? Thou shalt know.

23 For perfume mix meal & honey & thick leavings of red wine: then oil of Abramelin and olive oil, and afterward soften & smooth down with rich fresh blood!

24 The best blood is of the moon, monthly: then the fresh blood of a child, or dropping from the

host of heaven: then of enemies; then
of the priest or of the worshippers: last of
some beast, no matter what.

25 This burn: of this make cakes & eat unto
me. This hath also another use; let it be
laid before me, and kept thick with perfumes
of your orison: it shall become full of beetles
as it were and creeping things sacred unto me.

26 These slay, naming your enemies & they shall
fall before you.

27 Also these shall breed lust & power of lust in
you at the eating thereof.

28 Also ye shall be strong in war.

29 Moreover, be they long kept, it is better; for they swell with my force. All before me.

30 My altar is of open brass work: burn thereon in silver or gold.

31 There cometh a rich man from the West who shall pour his gold upon thee.

32 From gold forge steel:

33 Be ready to fly or to smite.

34 But your holy place shall be untouched throughout the centuries: though with fire and sword it be burnt down & shattered, yet an invisible house there standeth and shall stand until the fall of the Great

Equinox, when Hrumachis shall arise and the double-wanded one assume my throne and place. Another prophet shall arise, and bring fresh fever from the skies; another woman shall wake the lust & worship of the Snake; another soul of God and beast shall mingle in the globed priest; another sacrifice shall stain the tomb; another king shall reign; and blessing no longer be poured To the Hawk-headed mystical Lord!

35 The half of the word of Heru-ra-ha, called Hoor-pa-kraat and Ra-Hoor-Khut.

36 Then said the prophet unto the God.

37 "I adore thee in the song
"I am the Lord of Thebes" &c from Vellum book
———— "fill me"

38 So that thy light is in me & its red flame
is as a sword in my hand to push thy
order. There is a secret door that I shall
make to establish thy way in all the quarters
(these are the adorations, as thou hast written)
as it is said

"The light is mine" &c
from vellum book to "Ra-Hoor-Khuit"

39 All this. and a book to say how thou
didst come hither and a reproduction of
this ink and paper for ever — for in it is
the word secret & not only in the English —
and they comment upon this the Book of the Law
shall be printed beautifully in red ink and
black upon beautiful paper made by hand;
and to each man and woman that thou
meetest, were it but to dine or to drink
at them, it is the Law to give. Then they
shall chance to abide in this bliss or no;
it is no odds. Do this quickly!

40 But the work of the comment? That is easy; and

Hadit burning in My heart shall make swift
and secure My pen.

41. Establish at My Kaaba at a clerk-house:
all must be done well and with business
way.

42. The ordeals Thou shalt oversee Thyself, save only
the blind ones. Refuse none, but thou
shalt know & destroy the traitors. I am
Ra - Hoor - Khuit; and I am powerful to protect
my servant. Success is thy proof: argue not;
convert not: talk not overmuch. Them
that seek to entrap thee, to overthrow thee, them
attack without pity or quarter & destroy them
utterly. Swift as a trodden serpent turn.

and strike! Be thou deadlier than he!

42 Drag down their souls to awful torment: laugh at their fear: spit upon them!

43 Let the Scarlet Woman beware! If pity and compassion and tenderness visit her heart if she leave my work to toy with old sweetnesses then shall my vengeance be known. I will slay me her child: I will alienate her heart: I will cast her out from men: as a shrinking and despised whore shall she crawl through dusk wet streets, and die cold and an-hungered.

44. But let her raise herself in pride. Let her follow me in my way. Let her work the work of wickedness! Let her kill her heart! Let her be loud and adulterous; let her be covered with jewels and rich garments, and let her be shameless before all men!

45 Then will I lift her to pinnacles of power: then will I breed from her a child mightier than all the kings of the earth. I will fill her with joy: with my force shall she see & strike at the worship of Nu. she shall achieve Hadit.

46. I am the warrior Lord of the Forties: the
Eighties cower before me, & are abased
I will bring you to victory & joy: I will be
at your arms in battle & ye shall
delight to slay. Success is your proof;
courage is your armour; go on, go on, in
my strength & ye shall turn not back for
any.

47 This book shall be translated into all
tongues: but always with the original in
the writing of the Beast; for in the

chance shape of the letters and their
position to one another: in these are mysteries
that no Beast shall divine. Let him
not seek to try: but one cometh after
him, whence I say not, who shall
discover the key of it all. Then
this line drawn is a key: then this
circle squared ⊕ in its failure is a
key also. And Abrahadabra. It shall
be his child & that strangely. Let him not
seek after this; for thereby alone can he
fall from it.

48 Now this mystery of the letters is done, and I want to go on to the holier place.

49 I am in a secret fourfold word, the blasphemy against all gods of men.

50 Curse them! Curse them! Curse them!

51 With my Hawk's head I peck at the eyes of Jesus as he hangs upon the cross

52 I flap my wings in the face of Mohammed & blind him

53 With my claws I tear out the flesh of the Indian and the Buddhist, Mongol and Din.

54 Bahlasti! Ompehda! I spit on your

crapulous creeds.

55 Let Mary inviolate be torn upon wheels: for her sake let all chaste women be utterly despised among you.

56 Also for beauty's sake and love!

57 Despise also all cowards: professional soldiers who dare not fight, but play; all fools despise!

58 But the keen and the proud, the royal and the lofty; ye are brothers.

59 As brothers fight ye.

60 There is no law beyond Do what thou wilt.

61 There is an end of the word of the God

enthroned in Ra's seat, lightening the girders of the soul.

62 To Me do ye reverence; to me come ye through tribulation of ordeal, which is bliss.

63 The fool readeth this Book of the Law, and its comment & he understandeth it not.

64 Let him come through the first ordeal & it will be to him as silver

65 Through the second gold

66 Through the third, stones of precious water.

67 Through the fourth, ultimate sparks of the intimate fire.

68 Yet to all it shall seem beautiful. Its
enemies who say not so, are mere liars.

69 There is success

70 I am the Hawk-Headed Lord of Silence
& of Strength; my nemyss shrouds the
night-blue sky.

71 Hail! ye twin warriors about the pillars of
the world! for your time is nigh at hand

72 I am the Lord of the Double Wand of Power
the wand of the ~~Coph~~ Force of Coph Nia— ~~I~~ but my
left hand is empty, for I have crushed

an Universe & nought remains.

73 Paste the sheets from right to left and from top to bottom: then behold!

74 There is a splendour in my name hidden and glorious, as the sun of midnight is ever the son

75 The ending of the words is the Word Abrahadabra.

The Book of the Law is Written
    and Concealed.
        Aum. Ha.